HANDKERCHIEF
TRICKS

BRUCE SMITH

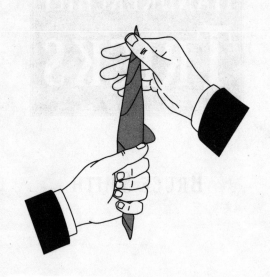

GLOSSARY OF TERMS

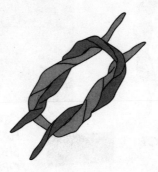

TWISTING A HANDKERCHIEF INTO A "ROPE"

REEF KNOT

CORNER OF A
HANDKERCHIEF
SHOWING THE
OPENING IN
THE HEM

FINGER PALM
OF A COIN

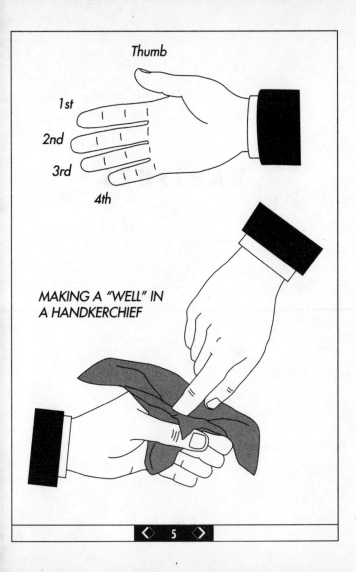

Thumb

1st

2nd

3rd

4th

MAKING A "WELL" IN
A HANDKERCHIEF

VANISHES

Effect *The magician ties a knot in the centre of a silk handkerchief. When the spectators blow on the knot it simply melts away.*

Requirements *A silk handkerchief or scarf 45 x 45cm/18 x 18in.*

Preparation *None.*

● ● ● ● ● ● ● ● ● ● ● ● ● ● ● ● ● ●

1 Hold the handkerchief by diagonally opposite corners between the first and second fingers of the left hand (end A) and the right hand (end B). Twist the handkerchief into a "rope" as shown in illustration 1.

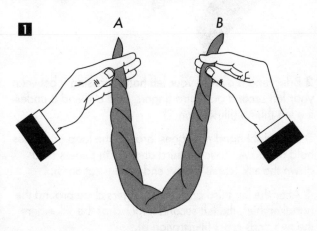

1   A   B

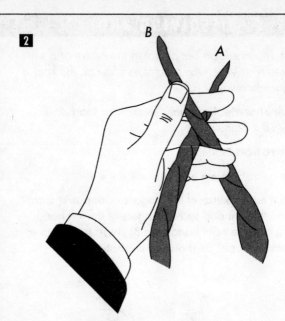

2 Bring end B over to your left hand, passing it between your left second and third fingers, and clip end B under the left thumb (illustration 2).

3 Your right hand now goes through the loop and takes hold of end A. Your left third and fourth fingers hold down the silk "rope" below end A (illustration 3).

4 After the left third and fourth fingers close around the handkerchief, the left second finger clips the silk where the two ends cross (illustration 3).

5 Pull end A through the loop with your right hand. End B is held tightly between the left thumb and first finger. The left third and fourth fingers release their grip around the silk as your left second finger hooks and pulls the lower portion of end B through the loop (illustration 4).

6 As you pull on end A a knot will form around the loop held by the second finger of the left hand. Remove your left second finger from inside the loop when the knot is tight enough to hold its own shape. This appears to be a genuine knot, but it is actually a slip knot.

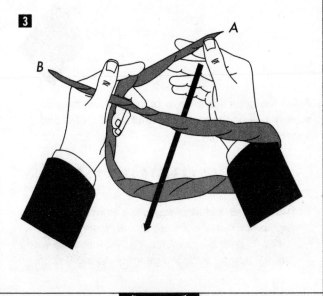

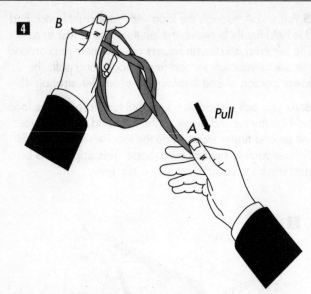

4

B

Pull

A

7 Ask the audience to blow at the knot. As they do, secretly pull on the ends. The knot will dissolve and appear to melt away.

ADE DUVAL (1898-1965)

Many magicians use silk handkerchief in their performances, but the American magician Ade Duval was one the few to create an entire act of "Silken Sorcery". With this unique act he travelled the world performing in exclusive glamourous night spots.

Effect *The magician pushes a silk handkerchief into his closed fist. After a suitable mystical pass the magician slowly opens his fist to show that the handkerchief has vanished!*

Requirements *A small hollow ball (a table tennis ball is ideal), a length of cord elastic, a safety pin and a silk handkerchief.*

Preparation *You will need to make a special prop known as a "pull". Cut a hole in one side of the ball large enough for the handkerchief to be pushed inside. Attach the ball to one end of the elastic and attach the safety pin to the other end (illustration 1). Pin the safety pin on the inside left of your jacket (illustration 2).*

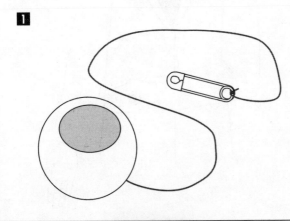

You will have to adjust the length of the cord elastic so that when it is stretched, the ball can be held comfortably in your right hand. When you release the ball the elastic should pull it up into your jacket. You need to experiment to get the right length of elastic for you.

Prepare by pinning the elastic inside your jacket as already described, and stretching the elastic so that you can hold the ball concealed in your closed right hand with the opening at the top (illustration 2).

● ● ● ● ● ● ● ● ● ● ● ● ● ● ● ● ● ●

1 Display the handkerchief and push it inside your closed fist, ensuring it goes inside the ball (illustration 3).

2 Wave your empty hand over your closed fist, at the same time releasing the ball, allowing it to shoot quickly inside your jacket, taking the handkerchief with it.

3 After a sufficient build-up you can slowly open your hand to show that it is completely empty.

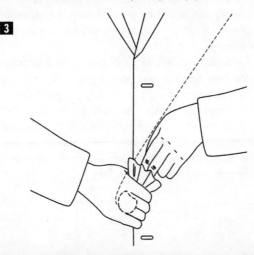

TOP TIPS FOR TRICKSTERS

Magic with coloured silk handkerchiefs is ideal for entertaining young children because it is bright, bold and uses a prop which they can all relate to.

Effect *A coin, ring or card is wrapped in a handkerchief and then vanishes!*

Requirements *Two identical pocket handkerchiefs, preferably with a colourful pattern or design.*

Preparation *The two handkerchiefs are made into a special "vanishing" handkerchief. This type of prop is known among magicians as a utility prop, because it is a specially made item that can be used for many different effects.*

Sew the handkerchiefs together along the four edges, leaving the hem open at one corner (point A in illustration 1). This opening should be slightly bigger than the object you intend to vanish. Then sew the handkerchiefs together to form a V-shaped pocket inside the handkerchiefs (illustration 2). The point of the V should be just below the middle of the handkerchiefs so that the object inside will naturally fall to the middle.

A

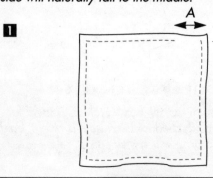

1

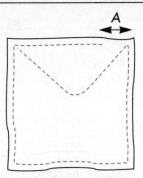

To give you an example of how to use the vanisher we will assume you want vanish a borrowed coin. Prepare by inserting a duplicate of the coin you intend to use inside the secret pocket (illustration 3).

● ● ● ● ● ● ● ● ● ● ● ● ● ● ●

1 Hold the handkerchief by the corners at the top of the sewn V (due to the nature of the material the audience will be unable to see where it has been sewn). Drape the handkerchief over your open empty left palm so that the hidden coin rests on your hand.

2 Borrow a coin and place it directly on top of the secret hidden coin.

3 With your right hand pick up both coins together – the borrowed one and, through the layer of material, the hidden coin. Turn everything upside down so that the handkerchief covers the coins and your hand. Hang on to

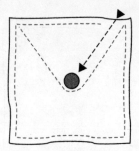

the hidden coin and allow the borrowed coin to slip into the palm of your hand where you can keep it concealed.

4 Ask a member of the audience to hold the coin through the handkerchief. They will feel the coin inside the handkerchief and hold it believing it to be the borrowed coin. When they have taken hold of the handkerchief and coin, allow your right hand to drop naturally to your side with the borrowed coin concealed in your curled fingers. You can secretly dispose of it in your pocket or load it somewhere to be reproduced later.

5 To vanish the coin hold one corner of the handkerchief and pull it from the spectator's grasp. They will feel the coin being pulled from their fingers, but fail to see it fall. It looks as though the coin has magically vanished in mid-air!

This is a very effective vanish and can be used in many other effects.

Effect *The magician makes a cone out of newspaper and pushes a silk handkerchief inside with a magic wand. The magician tears the newspaper into pieces to show that the silk handkerchief has completely vanished!*

Requirements *A newspaper, a silk handkerchief and a special magic wand (see "Preparation").*

Preparation *As the title of the effect suggests, it is the magic wand which makes the handkerchief disappear. To make this you will need a long thin hollow tube, plus a length of thin dowelling. Glue a circle of black card slightly larger than the diameter of the tube to the end of the dowelling (see illustration 1). Paint the tube black and white so that it looks like a magic wand.*

● ● ● ● ● ● ● ● ● ● ● ● ● ● ●

1

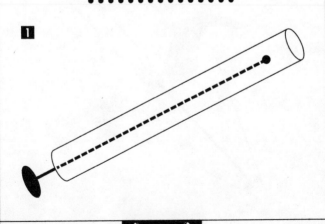

1 Form the newspaper into a cone. Rattle the magic wand inside the cone to prove it is empty. Secretly allow the rod to slide out and remain inside the cone. Drape the handkerchief over the mouth of the cone.

2 Using the magic wand you appear to push the silk down into the cone. In reality the wand slides over the rod and the rod and handkerchief are pushed up inside the hollow wand.

3 Remove the wand from the cone (with the rod and handkerchief tucked inside it) and set the wand down to one side.

5 Say the magic words and tear open the newspaper cone to show that it is completely empty!

2

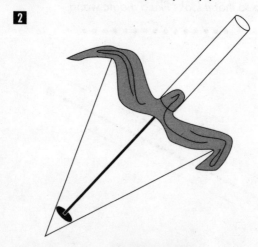

ANIMATION

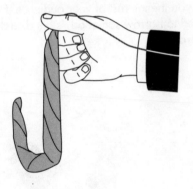

Effect *The magician hypnotises a handkerchief and it moves mysteriously as though obeying commands.*

Requirements *A pocket handkerchief.*

Preparation *None.*

• • • • • • • • • • • • • • •

1 Claim to be able to hypnotise any pocket handkerchief. This is an impressive and unusual claim and will surely gain you the interest of your audience. Explain that you need to borrow somebody's handkerchief to be "put into a trance".

2 When you have borrowed a handkerchief spread it out flat on the table (it always worth having a handkerchief of your own in your pocket in case nobody in your audience has one in a suitable state!).

3 Grab the top lefthand corner of the handkerchief with your left fingers and thumb, and with your right fingers and thumb hold the left edge about halfway down. Lift up the handkerchief and twist it between your hands to form a tightly twisted "rope".

4 Hold the handkerchief up vertically with your right hand at the top and the left hand below (illustration 1).

5 Keep hold with the right hand and move your left hand to a position about halfway up. As you do this make sure the handkerchief remains tightly twisted.

2

6 Pull the handkerchief tight between your hands and slowly let go with your right hand. The handkerchief will remain rigid as though hypnotised. "There you are," you say, "completely under my control!"

7 Gaze at the handkerchief and say in your most commanding tones, "Forward, forward, forward!" At the same time gently move your left thumb down the handkerchief and it will lean towards you.

8 Continue, "Back, back, back!" and move your left thumb back up the handkerchief. It will gradually slowly move away from you.

9 Repeat this a number of times, then move your left hand to hold the handkerchief horizontal to show it is rigid and completely in a trance. Say, "But it can be woken. On the count of three, when I snap my fingers it will wake up and will be unable to remember any of the things that have happened in the last few minutes!"

10 Return the handkerchief to its vertical position, click your fingers and flick open the handkerchief. Return it to its owner with a warning that it may never be the same again!

TOP TIPS FOR TRICKSTERS
Magic with silk handkerchiefs is often best when performed "silently" to a musical background, without the usual magician's patter.

This is not a baffling trick, but an amusing "bit of business" to perform either between tricks or to entertain a group of children at a social event. It would be a nice follow up to the "Hypnotised Hanky".

Effect The magician transforms a pocket handkerchief into a doll-like replica of a ballet dancer. At the magician's command the figure seems to come alive with a high kicking spinning flourish!

Requirements A pocket handkerchief.

Preparation None.

● ● ● ● ● ● ● ● ● ● ● ● ● ● ●

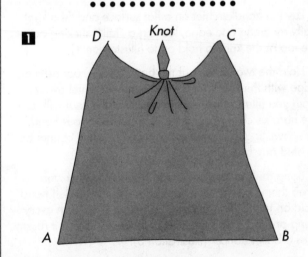

1 Lay the handkerchief on a flat surface and tie a knot halfway along one edge, leaving a "tail" sticking out of the top of the knot to hold on to (illustration 1).

2 Hold the two corners of the bottom edge, opposite the edge with the knot in it. Twirl the handkerchief away from you (illustration 2). The weight of the knot will spin the handkerchief around the hem between your hands. Keep twisting the handkerchief tightly, until it cannot be twisted any further.

3 Bring the two corners in your hands together and grab them both in your right hand. With your left hand hold on to the "tail" sticking out of the knot. Turn every-thing around – with the knot at the top – so that it resembles a ballet dancer (illustration 3).

4 By moving your hands you can animate the "ballet dancer" so that she swings her hips or bows. If you let go of one corner with the right hand you can make her perform a high kick (illustration 4), and then go into a dramatic spin, until you are just left with a hanky with a knot in it! A ballet dancer's career is always short!

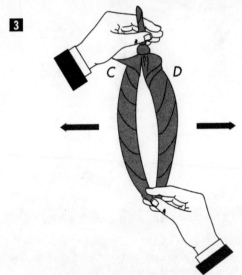

3

C   D

4

HOUDIN AND THE KING'S HANKIES

During Robert Houdin's Command performance at the palace of King Louis Phillipe he borrowed six handkerchiefs. The King requested that they should be magically sent under the last orange tree outside the palace. A guard was sent to the tree while Houdin vanished the bundle of hankies. An iron box was found buried under the selected tree and locked inside were the six borrowed handkerchiefs!

Effect *The magician ties a knot in the middle of a handkerchief. The handkerchief begins to move like a snake and unties the knot!*

Requirements *A silk handkerchief 45 x 45cm/18 x18in and 180cm/6ft of fine black nylon thread .*

Preparation *Attach one end of the thread to one corner of the handkerchief. Attach the other end to your table. Fold the handkerchief and place it on your table alongside the length of thread.*

• • • • • • • • • • • • • • • •

1 Pick up the handkerchief and stand about 1m/3ft to the side of the table. Hold the handkerchief by the corner knotted to the thread. We will call this end A. The thread should pass under your right arm to the table

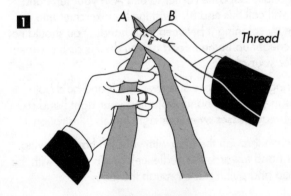

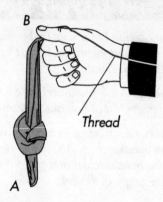

2

B

Thread

A

top. Do not worry about anybody seeing the thread. The attention of the audience is on you and what you do with the handkerchief.

2 What you do with the handkerchief is to take the diagonally opposite corner to end A in your left hand (we will call this end B). Twist the handkerchief into a rope by spinning it between your hands. You should not get caught up in the thread as you do this as it passes under your arm.

3 Bring end A across and over end B and hold both ends in your right hand, adjusting your right hand so the thread passes over your right thumb (illustration 1).

4 Reach through the loop with your left hand (moving your hand towards the audience), grasp end A with the thread and pull it back through the loop.

5 Pull your hands apart slowly so that a knot forms in the centre (illustration 2). Unknown to the audience the thread passes through the loop in the knot. It is important the thread runs over your right thumb.

6 Release end A, so the handkerchief is held in the right hand. The thread is attached to the bottom corner A of the handkerchief and passes up through the knot, over your right thumb and across the table.

7 So if you move your right arm forward, the thread will pull end A up and through the knot (illustration 3). Gently move forward to pull end A up to your right hand. The knot will appear to melt away. When end A reaches your hand, release your hold of end B and grasp end A (illustration 4). Drop the handkerchief back on to your table, concluding your performance of the world's first untying knot!

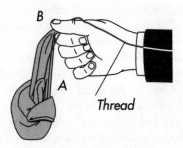

B

A

Thread

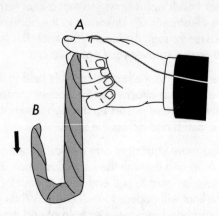

This is a stunning visual effect that is in the repertoire of many of the world's best professional magicians. It is important that you spend plenty of time practising, rehearsing and mastering this effect before you attempt to show it to anyone.

It is also possible to perform this effect without using a table. Instead of attaching the thread to the table you use a shorter length of thread, and attach one end to the handkerchief and the other end to a bead. The bead will dangle down to the floor. After you have tied the knot, put your right foot on the bead. The only other difference in the trick is that you move your right arm upwards instead of forwards to untie the knot.

   This method enables you to perform the effect almost impromptu.

PENETRATIONS

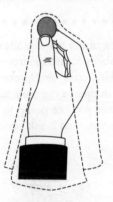

Effect *A silk handkerchief – representing the world famous escape artiste Harry Houdini – escapes from a sealed glass tumbler.*

Requirements *Two different coloured silk handkerchiefs, a large silk scarf, 25cm/10in of cotton thread, a glass tumbler and an elastic band.*

Preparation *Tie the cotton thread to one corner of the handkerchief that you want to "escape".*

●●●●●●●●●●●●●●●●

1 Tell the audience about the exploits of the Great Houdini and his ability to escape from any confinement – prison cell, packing case, straitjacket or handcuffs. Explain that your audience are very fortunate because for the first time ever you are going to introduce the re-incarnation of Houdini – as a silk handkerchief!

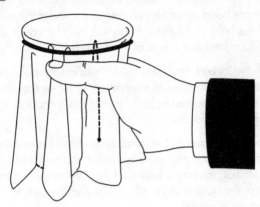

2 Display the "Houdini silk" to the audience and push it down into the bottom of the empty tumbler. As you do this make sure that you leave the thread hanging outside the glass.

3 Introduce the second handkerchief as a prison guard and stuff it into the tumbler on top of the first handkerchief (illustration 1).

4 To make extra sure that the handkerchief is unable to escape, throw the scarf over the mouth of the tumbler and hold it in place with the elastic band (illustration 2). You could call this the padded cell – or perhaps this is taking the analogy a bit too far!

5 Now tell the audience that this escape used to take 30 minutes! But today you intend to double that time! After a suitable build-up of tension, reach up under the scarf and take hold of the thread (this will be a lot easier if you tied a knot in the end of the thread).

6 Pull the thread, and the Houdini silk will be pulled out of the glass. You need to experiment to make sure that you are using an elastic band that is loose enough to enable you to do this.

7 Once the corner of the handkerchief has been pulled past the rubber band, grab hold of it and pull it sharply downwards, making it look as if the silk has penetrated through the bottom of the glass. Houdini lives on to escape once again!

3

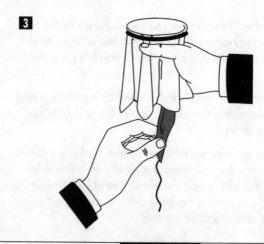

This is based on the "Dissolving Knot" and it is highly recommended that you learn and perfect that effect before attempting this one.

Effect *The magician displays two silk handkerchiefs, which are then twisted into ropes. A spectator holds one outstretched between his hands. The handkerchiefs are securely knotted around each other, creating two knotted linked loops of silk. Like the classic "Chinese Linking Rings" the handkerchiefs seem to melt apart with their knots still intact.*

1

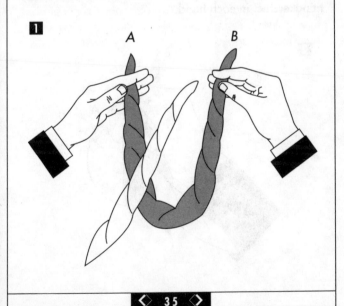

Requirements *Two silk handkerchiefs 45 x 45cm/18 x 18in, preferably of contrasting colours.*

Preparation *None.*

● ● ● ● ● ● ● ● ● ● ● ● ● ● ● ●

1 Hold the first handkerchief by its diagonally opposite corners and twist it into a rope. Hand it to a member of the audience, requesting them to hold on tightly to the two ends.

2 Twist the second handkerchief and thread it underneath the first (illustration 1). Hold an end of your handkerchief in each hand.

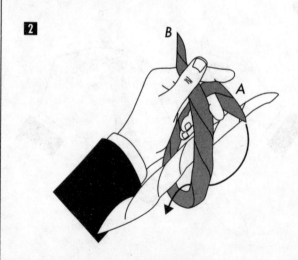

3

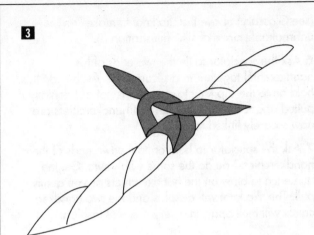

3 Move the righthand end (end B) over to the left hand and clip the two ends exactly as in the "Dissolving Knot" (illustration 2). Insert your right hand through the loop and grab end A. Pull this end back through the loop to form the "Dissolving Knot".

4 Pull the two ends of your rope in opposite directions to tighten to the knot. As you do this, keep your left second finger in the small loop. When the knot becomes tight you can slide out your left finger and the knot will hold itself together.

5 Loop your handkerchief underneath the spectator's handkerchief again and tie a regular secure reef knot (see Glossary) above the slip knot to make "an unbreakable circle of silk" (illustration 3).

6 Ask the spectator to tie the two ends of his handkerchief together in a secure knot. As they do this, hold on to the slip knot to ensure it is not accidentally pulled apart. It seems that the two handkerchiefs are now securely linked together.

7 Ask the spectator to hold on to the two ends of their handkerchief. You do the same with yours. Get the audience to blow on the handkerchiefs as you gently pull. The slip knot will dissolve and the two handkerchiefs will melt apart in a very magical fashion.

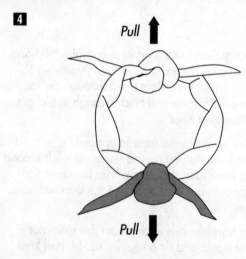

4

Pull ↑

Pull ↓

Effect *The magician sticks a pencil through the centre of a borrowed handkerchief without damaging it!*

Requirements *The largest handkerchief you can borrow (a cloth table napkin will do), a pencil 8cm/3in long and a piece of newspaper 30 x 30cm/12 x 12in.*

Preparation *None.*

•••••••••••••••••

1 Invite two spectators to assist you. Have them each hold on to two corners of the borrowed handkerchief and stretch it between them so that it is parallel with the floor.

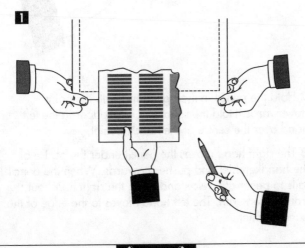

2 The right hand holds the pencil underneath the hanky, the finger holds the pencil secretly. When the secret cloth is pressed down, and the pencil is held point up, the secret pencil is the edge of the

2

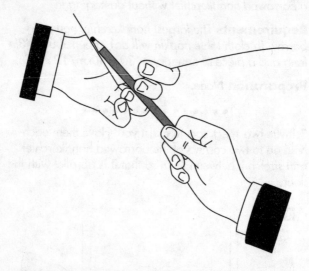

2 Hold the pencil in the right hand with the point downwards. Hold the square of newspaper in the left hand over the centre of the handkerchief.

3 The right hand moves the pencil under the centre of the handkerchief and pushes upwards. When the pencil fails to penetrate, relax and bring the right hand out from underneath. The left hand moves to the edge of the handkerchief.

3

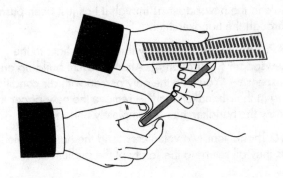

4 Look at the pencil and say, "Of course, the pencil should be pointed end up." Turn the pencil around.

5 As the right hand moves back under the handkerchief you perform the all-important secret move. The left second and third fingers clip the pencil (illustration 2). This action is covered by the newspaper.

6 The right hand does not pause, but continues to move underneath to the centre of the handkerchief as though it still contained the pencil.

7 The left hand moves forward on top of the handkerchief back to the centre.

8 Through the fabric the right hand grips the blunt end of the pencil. With the left hand, push the newspaper down over the pencil (illustration 3). The pencil tears a hole in the newspaper as though it has just been pushed through the handkerchief.

9 Pull the pencil all the way through the hole in the newspaper (illustration 4). After sufficient build-up and suspense – "You'll be the only person with air condition-ing in their handkerchief!" – remove the newspaper to show the handkerchief is completely unharmed!

10 Thank your two volunteers (and the handkerchief!) as they all return to the safety of the audience!

4

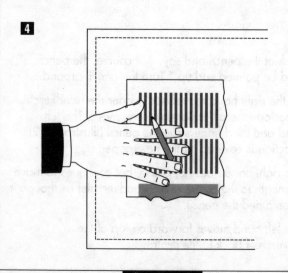

Effect *A coin and a handkerchief are both borrowed from members of the audience. The coin visibly passes through the centre of the handkerchief, leaving it undamaged!*

Requirements *A coin and a handkerchief (both can be borrowed).*

Preparation *None.*

● ● ● ● ● ● ● ● ● ● ● ● ● ● ● ●

1 Display the coin at the tips of the right thumb and first two fingers so that the audience see one side of the coin. Your left hand drapes the handkerchief over the coin and right hand so that the coin is under the approximate centre of the handkerchief (illustration 1).

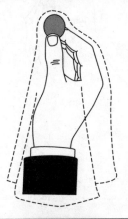

2 As the left hand is adjusting the handkerchief over the coin, your left thumb secretly lifts a bit of cloth behind the coin and folds it behind the right thumb. When you remove your left hand you will have two layers of cloth clipped between your right thumb and the back of the coin (illustration 2), preparing you for the secret move.

3 With your left hand grab the front edge of the handkerchief and lift it back and over the coin. This displays the coin still in position under the centre of the handkerchief. When you cover the coin again your left

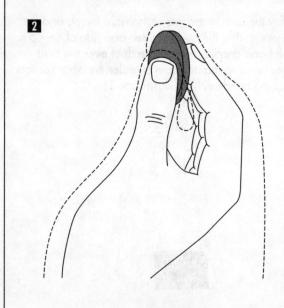

hand takes both edges of the handkerchief over the coin (illustration 3). Now your right thumb is holding the coin outside the handkerchief. The clipped piece of cloth prevents the handkerchief falling away after you have done this (illustration 4).

4 With your left hand, grip the coin from above through the layers of the handkerchief. Your right hand now lets go of the coin and twists the lower part of the handkerchief to reveal the shape of the coin (illustration 5).

5 Slowly push the coin upwards with your right hand, as your left hand takes the edge of the coin – as it magically penetrates through the handkerchief.

4

5

◇ SHRINKING COIN ◇

Effect *A coin, a handkerchief and a finger ring are all borrowed from members of the audience. The coin is wrapped in the centre of the handkerchief, and the ring threaded over all four corners to trap it inside. Despite this secure set-up the coin manages to pass through the ring and escape from inside the handkerchief – much to the audience's amazement!*

Requirements *A handkerchief, a large coin and a finger ring – the effect is much more impressive if all these items are borrowed from members of the audience, but it is worth having your own standing by ready to use if necessary. If you do have to use your own props, have them examined by the audience before you begin the effect.*

Preparation *There is no specific preparation for this effect, but it is highly recommended that you master the "Coin Through Handkerchief" effect before attempting to perform this one.*

● ● ● ● ● ● ● ● ● ● ● ● ● ● ● ● ●

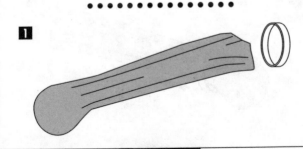

1 Have the handkerchief, coin and finger ring examined by the audience. Then collect them together and invite two members of the audience up to assist you.

2 Display the coin and wrap it in the handkerchief as described in the "Coin Through Handkerchief" effect so that the coin is held outside the handkerchief (illustration 1). Twist the lower part of the handkerchief to reveal the shape of the apparently trapped coin (but do not perform the penetration).

3 Hold the coin through the handkerchief in the left hand so that the coin is resting flat against the left fingers. The "open" side (which would reveal the coin) is resting against the fingertips.

4 Have a spectator thread the finger ring over all four corners of the handkerchief. As they do this hold the coin tightly with the left hand, and with the right hand hold the handkerchief just above the coin to prevent it unwrapping.

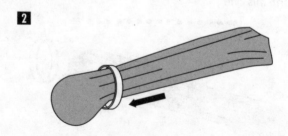

5 Have the spectator slide the ring down the handkerchief until it reaches the coin (illustration 2). The ring will lock the coin in position and prevent the handkerchief unwrapping. You can now ask two spectators to each hold two corners of the handkerchief so that it is parallel with the floor (illustration 3) while you let go of the coin. The coin and ring are both below the handkerchief.

6 Point out the situation to audience – the coin is trapped in the centre of the handkerchief by the ring. It cannot escape as the hole in the middle of the ring is much smaller than the coin.

7 Reach under the handkerchief with both hands. With your left hand slide the ring up the handkerchief to give you sufficient slack to release the coin into your right hand (illustration 4). Until the end of the trick your left hand remains under the handkerchief holding on to the ring and the centre of the handkerchief, so that your spectators believe the coin is still trapped inside.

8 Conceal the coin in your right hand in the finger palm position. To finger palm a coin, simply clip it at the base of the fingers by slightly closing your hand until the coin is held securely in position. (When you hold your hands naturally they are usually slightly closed.) The audience believe the coin is trapped in the handkerchief and they have no reason to suspect it is anywhere else. If you do not draw attention to your right hand, your audience won't bother about it either.

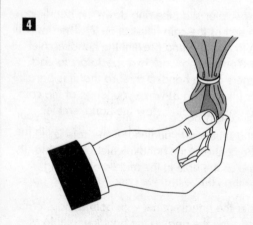

9 Bring your apparently empty right hand over the top of the handkerchief to the middle over the "well" in the centre. Your right hand secretly releases the finger-palmed coin into this well in the handkerchief. Under the handkerchief the left fingers catch the coin and grip it through the fabric.

10 Wave your right hand over the centre in a mystical fashion as though you are performing a "magical pass" over the well. This was your reason for moving your hand to the centre of the handkerchief.

11 Ask the spectators to slowly pull on their corners of the handkerchief. Very slowly with your left hand release the coin. It will appear to rise up out of the centre of the handkerchief as though it is passing through the centre of the ring. This is a very magical moment when done slowly and should get a great round of applause from your audience – and a gasp of amazement from your two "hanky holders".

12 Allow your two assistants to continue pulling on their corners until the handkerchief is stretched flat between them with the coin lying on top in the centre. Bring your left hand out from underneath the handkerchief with the borrowed finger ring to show that it is undamaged. You point out that the impossible must have occurred. The only explanation can be that the coin "shrank" to pass through the ring and then grew back to its original size. You can finish by saying, "I've heard of deflating currency but this is ridiculous!"

COLOUR CHANGES

Effect *The magician displays a handkerchief. As the magician's hand is passed over it the handkerchief changes colour.*

Requirements *Two different coloured silk handkerchiefs, a metal ring with diameter 2.5cm/1in and sewing equipment.*

Preparation *Place one handkerchief on top of the other and sew them together just above the centre with a line of stitching about 5cm/2in long. Sew the top corner of the rear handkerchief to the far side of the metal ring. Poke the top corner A of the upper handkerchief through the ring (illustration 1).*

Fold up the lower corner B of the upper handkerchief and sew it to the near side of the metal ring (illustration 2). Fold the set-up in half lengthwise so that the lower handkerchief covers the folded top handkerchief (illustration 3). Sew the two sides of the outer handkerchief together, ensuring that the inner silk does not bulge out too much, but lies flat.

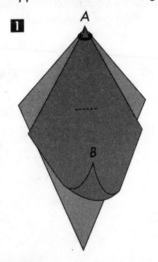

Grasp the tip A of the inner silk through the ring and pull the ring down. This will transpose the handkerchiefs, exposing the inner silk and concealing the outer one. Sew up the sides of the now outer handkerchief to prevent the inner silk from being seen.

• • • • • • • • • • • • • • • • •

1 Display the handkerchief to your audience.

2 With the left hand grasp the tip of the handkerchief sticking out of the ring.

3 Pull the ring down over the silk with the right hand. To the audience it appears that the handkerchief changes colour as your hand passes over it (illustration 4). As the handkerchief changes colour, shake it slightly.

2

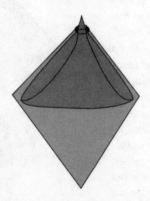

4 You can end the effect there or turn the handkerchief upside down and repeat the process to restore the handkerchief to its original colour.

3

4

Effect *A red silk handkerchief with white borders is pulled through the hand and changes to a green silk handkerchief with white borders.*

Requirements *A white handkerchief, plus two slightly smaller ones, one red and the other green.*

Preparation *Make a special handkerchief by sewing the two coloured handkerchiefs one each side of the white one (illustration 1).*

● ● ● ● ● ● ● ● ● ● ● ● ● ● ●

1

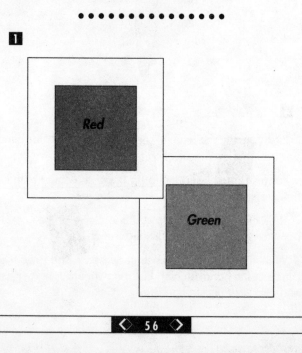

1 Pick up the handkerchief, displaying the red side, and spread it out over your open left hand.

2 Form your left hand into a fist under the cover of the handkerchief.

3 With the right forefinger push the centre of the handkerchief into the left fist (illustration 2).

4 With your right hand reach underneath and grab the centre of the handkerchief. Pull it down through your fist and into view (illustration 3).

5 The handkerchief is now green. Show the green side to the audience, making sure that you keep the red side hidden.

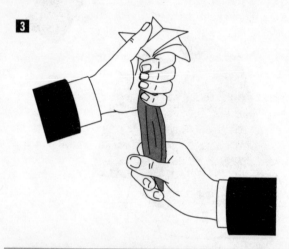

3

Effect *After the wave of a magic wand the magician produces a silk handkerchief from his hands, which were empty moments before. Another wave of the wand and the handkerchief changes colour!*

Requirements *A magic wand and two contrasting silk handkerchiefs – say, red and yellow.*

Preparation *Fold the four corners of each handkerchief to the centre. Then roll each one into a tube and wrap them alongside each other around one end of the wand (illustration 1). To perform this as an opener, hold the wand in your right hand, with your hand concealing the handkerchiefs. To perform later, set the wand on your table with other props covering the handkerchiefs.*

• • • • • • • • • • • • • • •

1

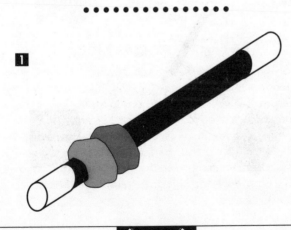

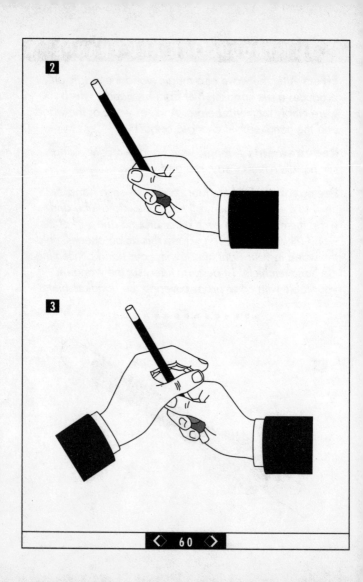

1 Begin with the wand in the right hand (illustration 2). Tap the empty left hand with the free end of the wand as you say, "My left hand is empty . . ."

2 Slide the left hand up the wand until the two hands meet (illustration 3). The left hand grasps the end of the wand, covering the two handkerchiefs. The wand pivots to the right and the right hand is shown to be empty as you say, ". . . and the right too."

3 The left hand keeps hold of the lower of the two handkerchiefs, as the right hand takes the wand back concealing the other handkerchief on the wand. We will assume the handkerchief in the left hand is red and the one still on the wand is yellow.

4

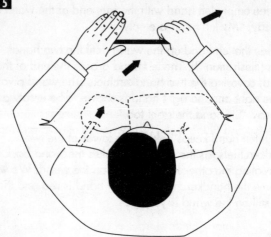

4 The right hand places the wand under the left arm so that the handkerchief is concealed under the left armpit and the free end sticks out in front (illustration 4).

5 The right hand points to the left hand, which reaches forward and snaps out the red silk handkerchief – apparently from nowhere!

6 When the applause from this production has died down, continue by rolling up the red handkerchief into a ball. This goes into your left hand while you make a magical pass with your right hand. Open your left hand to show that nothing has happened.

7 Roll the handkerchief up again, but this time keep it concealed in your right hand while pretending it is your closed left fist.

8 The right hand (holding the red handkerchief concealed) reaches for the free end of the wand and moves it down (illustration 5) behind your left arm (which acts as a screen) and into the left hand which opens briefly to secretly "steal" the yellow handkerchief from the end of the wand. The wand continues moving.

9 Wave the wand over the closed left fist and open it to show that the handkerchief has now changed colour.

When performed correctly this is a very baffling and convincing effect, but it is highly recommended that you rehearse it many times in front of a mirror to ensure that your timing is correct and that in step 8 the yellow handkerchief remains concealed from the audience.

HOUDIN AND HOUDINI

In 1856 Robert Houdin was sent by the French government to Algiers to quell the revolution by proving that French magic was stronger than African magic! On his return he wrote of his adventures in The Memoirs of Robert Houdin. Nearly 30 years later a young Hungarian boy in America read the book and decided to become a magician. He based his stage name on that of his hero – and became Houdini!

PRODUCTIONS

◇ THE ORGAN PIPES ◇

Effect After showing that two tubes are both completely empty, the magician produces silk handkerchiefs and ribbons from inside.

Requirements Two tubes about 30cm/12in high and 15cm/6in diameter, which fit one inside the other (it may be easiest to make the tubes to size using stiff paper held together with paper clips), a paper clip, about 15cm/6in of dark thread, elastic bands and your production "load" – ribbons and silk handkerchiefs.

1

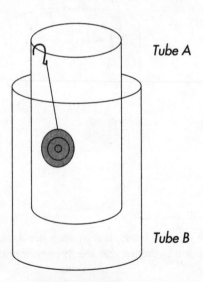

Tube A

Tube B

Preparation *Roll up the handkerchiefs and ribbons into a compact bundle and hold it together with the elastic bands. Bend the paper clip into an S-shaped hook. Attach one end of the thread to the hook and the other end to one of the elastic bands. Hook the clip over the top edge of the thinner tube (tube A) with the bundle dangling inside out of sight. We will call the wider of the two tubes tube B.*

Set tubes A and B next to each other on the table.

● ● ● ● ● ● ● ● ● ● ● ● ● ● ● ● ●

2

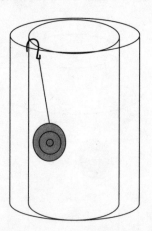

1 Pick up both tubes, one in each hand. Hold up tube B so that the audience can see through it and see that it is empty.

2 Slide tube A into the top of tube B, making sure that the hook clips on to the top of tube B (illustration 2).

3 Allow tube A to slide out of the bottom of tube B. The bundle should remain hanging out of sight inside tube B. You can now hold up tube A to show the audience that it is completely empty.

4 Slide tube A back into tube B from the bottom, so that the bundle is now hanging inside both tubes (illustration 3). Roll up your sleeves and show the audience that your hands are completely empty. Reach inside the tubes and remove the elastic bands from around the

3

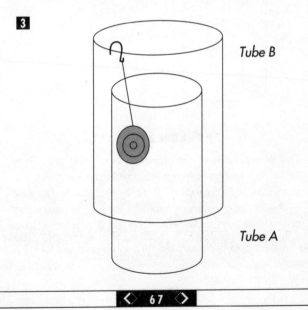

Tube B

Tube A

bundle. Dramatically remove the ribbons and handkerchiefs from inside the nested tubes (illustration 4).

4

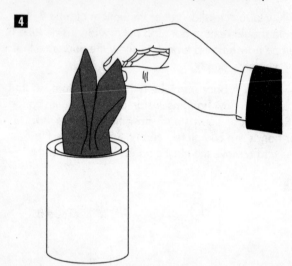

THE ZOMBIE BALL

This effect is one of the true classics of magic. A silver ball floats underneath a silk handkerchief without any visible means of support. At times it comes to balance at the top edge of the handkerchief before continuing its mysterious movements. This effect is a great piece of situation comedy when performed by Ali Bongo, the "Shriek" of Araby.

◇ APPEARING SILK HANKY ◇

Effect *This is a startling opening effect. The magician shows both hands empty. After making a grab in the air a silk handkerchief appears in the magician's hands!*

Requirements *A silk handkerchief about 45 x 45cm/18 x 18in.*

Preparation *Spread the handkerchief out flat on a table. Fold the four corners into the middle so that they almost touch (illustrations 1 and 2). Repeat, folding the four new corners into the centre. Continue folding until you have a bundle about 5cm/2in across.*

1

2

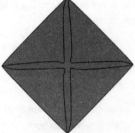

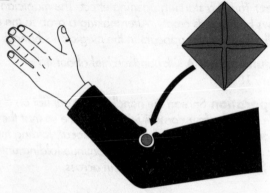

3

Place the folded handkerchief in the bend of your elbow (illustration 3) just before you begin your performance. If you keep your arm bent the handkerchief will remain concealed.

● ● ● ● ● ● ● ● ● ● ● ● ● ● ● ●

This effect is over in just a few seconds, but it appears to be quite magical.

1 Show the audience that both your hands are empty by wiggling your fingers.

2 Look upwards. Quickly reach up with both hands and, as you do this, straighten your arms. The handkerchief will be propelled into the air (illustration 4).

3 Catch the handkerchief between your hands. It seems to have appeared in mid-air.

4

ROBERT HOUDIN (1805-1871)

Robert Houdin was a French watchmaker who became a magician and the talk of Paris with his Soirées Fantastiques at his own specially-built theatre. He revolutionised magic and is credited as being "The Father of Modern Magic". He used his mechanical skills to build many of his effects. In one of the most famous, a lady's handkerchief was borrowed and vanished. Flowers and fruit appeared on a nearby orange tree. One of the oranges opened and two butterflies flew out carrying the borrowed handkerchief, which was then returned to its astonished owner.

Effect *The magician displays an arrow with a mind of its own – and then produces a handkerchief from inside.*

Requirements *A square sheet of thick paper, extra paper, invisible sellotape and a silk handkerchief.*

Preparation *Fold the piece of paper into quarters lengthwise. Stick an extra piece of paper on to one panel to make a secret pocket with a flap. Then make the paper into a tube by sticking two edges together with sellotape (illustrations 1 and 2). Hide the handkerchief inside the pocket. Flatten the tube down and cut it as shown in illustration 3 to make a nose and a tail.*

• • • • • • • • • • • • • • • •

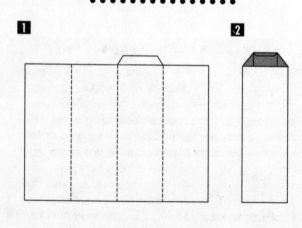

1　　　　　　　　　　　　**2**

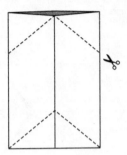

1 Show the arrow pointing to your left and tell your audience that they must never trust arrows as they might be pointing the wrong way.

2 Turn the arrow around so that it is pointing to the right. Say, "See, it is easy to move an arrow. Sometimes it changes direction so quickly it seems like magic!"

3 As you say this you squeeze the two outer edges together so that the tube opens out and folds flat the other way. The arrow is now pointing left again.

4 You can turn the arrow left and right by repeating step 3 as many times as you wish.

5 Finally conclude by saying, "Of course, you can't trust me – I'm a magician. I was just trying to pull the wool over your eyes!" As you say this, reach into the end of the arrow and pull the silk handkerchief out of the secret pocket (illustration 5).

4

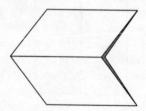

5

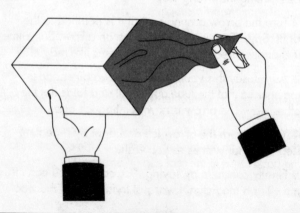

Effect *The magician shows the audience an ordinary handkerchief. He folds it in half and an egg rolls out from inside. He tips the egg into a basket. Another egg appears . . . and another . . . and another. This apparently unlimited number of eggs are shaken, one at a time, from the handkerchief into the basket. The magician sets the handkerchief down to one side, reaches into the basket, removes one egg and breaks it into a glass to prove it is real. Walking forward with the basket the magician throws the contents at the audience! To the audience's surprise – and relief – the eggs have been transformed into a basketful of confetti!*

Requirements *An opaque handkerchief 60 x 60cm/24 x 24in, a small basket, a plastic egg, a real egg, a glass, some thread to match the colour of the handkerchief and a supply of confetti.*

Preparation *Attach the plastic egg to one end of a piece of thread about 30cm/12in long. Attach the other end of the thread to the centre of one edge of the handkerchief, so that the egg hangs just below the centre of the handkerchief when the handkerchief is held up (illustration 2). Fill the basket with confetti and hide the real egg inside. Fold the handkerchief and place it next to the basket with the false egg resting on the confetti inside the basket next to the real egg (illustration 1).*

● ● ● ● ● ● ● ● ● ● ● ● ● ● ● ● ●

1

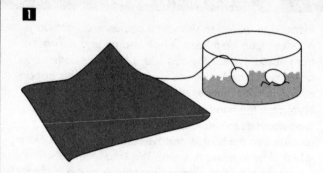

1 Lift up the handkerchief by the edge which does not have the thread attached. The egg will remain hidden in the basket while you show both sides of the handkerchief to the audience. Say, "As you can see, there are no chickens hidden in my handkerchief!" The audience will wonder what you are talking about. They will soon find out . . .

2 Lay the threaded hem of the handkerchief over the top of the basket so that it covers the plastic egg. Show that your hands are empty and roll up your sleeves, saying, "No chickens up my sleeves!"

TOP TIPS FOR TRICKSTERS

Magic with silk handkerchiefs is ideally suited for female magicians because the props involved have a definite "feminine" feel to them.

3 Pick up the handkerchief by the corners of the threaded hem and pull the hem tight between your hands. Lift the handkerchief straight up away from the basket and table. The thread will pull the egg out of the basket and it will dangle concealed behind the handkerchief (illustration 2).

4 Bring the top two corners together in your left hand (illustration 3), concealing the egg in the folds of the handkerchief. Your right hand holds the two lower corners together and moves up to the right until the folded handkerchief is held horizontally.

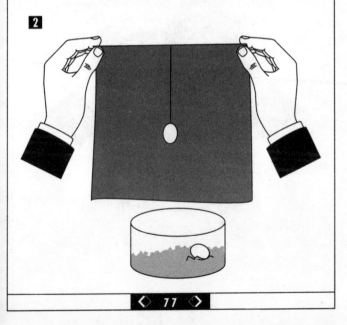

2

5 Move the handkerchief so that it is to your right of the basket. Lift your right hand slightly and shake the egg out of the handkerchief (illustration 4) so that it falls into the basket and lands on the confetti. Now the audience will understand all this talk of invisible chickens!

6 Rest the handkerchief back on top of the basket. The corners in the right hand go on the table in front of the basket. The right hand moves up to the left hand to take hold of one of the two corners being held in the left hand.

3

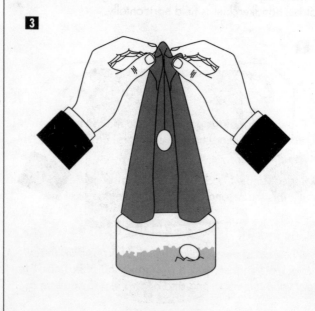

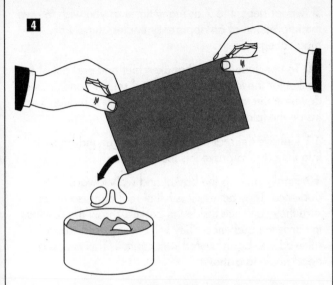

7 Draw your hands apart and raise the top two corners, again secretly lifting the egg out of the basket behind the handkerchief.

8 Repeat steps 4 and 5 to produce a second egg – really it is the second showing of the same one!

TOP TIPS FOR TRICKSTERS

When entertaining children with effects with different coloured handkerchiefs it is a good "bit of business" to get your colours wrong and allow them to correct you.

9 Repeat steps 4 to 7 as many times as you wish to give the impression of an apparently endless supply of magical eggs.

10 To conclude, lift the handkerchief and egg out of the basket for the last time (step 7) and set the handkerchief down on the table, ensuring that the egg is hidden inside the folds of the handkerchief.

11 Remove the real egg from the basket and break it into the glass to prove it is the real thing!

12 Finally pick up the basket and walk towards the audience. They believe it is full of real eggs, so make sure they can't see inside the basket. Throw the contents towards the audience. They will be surprised – and relieved – to be showered with confetti. This makes a good finale to a show!

HARRY BLACKSTONE (1885-1965)

Harry Blackstone toured the theatres of America in the mid 1900s with his spectacular illusion show. One of the highlights of his show was his "Haunted Hanky" effect, in which a borrowed handkerchief apparently became possessed by spirits and began moving and dancing around the stage! This effect is still performed today by his son, Harry Blackstone Jnr, who travels the world with his own illusion show keeping the name Blackstone up in lights.